Written by Julie Senatore

# All that We Learn... and Teach

Illustrated by Kimberlee Lada

Written by Julie Senatore

# All that
# We Learn...
# and Teach

Illustrated by Kimberlee Lada

# Dedication

This book is dedicated to the tiny fighters, the warriors of the NICU, whose strength defies their size. May your journey be filled with hope, healing, love and grace.  Spending time cuddling with you has given me some of the best moments of my life.

And to the nurses, the angels in scrubs, who tend to these precious lives with unwavering care and compassion. Your dedication and expertise are a beacon of hope for countless families.

A Heartfelt Thank You To
Jennifer And Jason Schafer For Believing In This Project.

As you begin your journey in life
Always know that you are a treasure!

You might not always think so,
but even as you face life's biggest challenges...

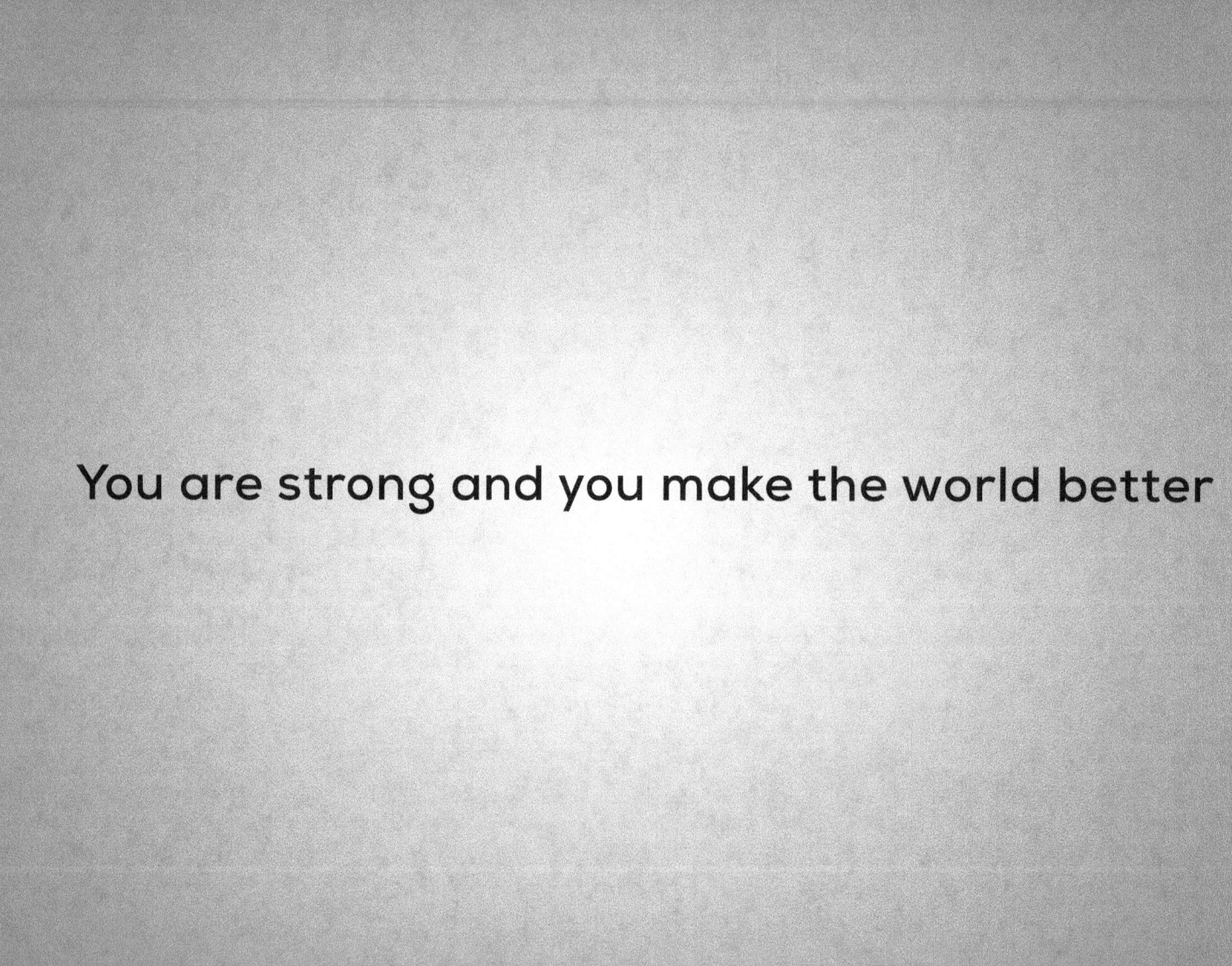
You are strong and you make the world better

It's true that sometimes we might wish for an easier path...

But every challenge we face gives
us the chance to learn...
... and to teach!

We learn that we can overcome ginormous obstacles...
...and teach patience in difficult situations

We learn to receive and extend grace to those who care for us.

We learn that the care we receive from others gives us the strength to help those in need.

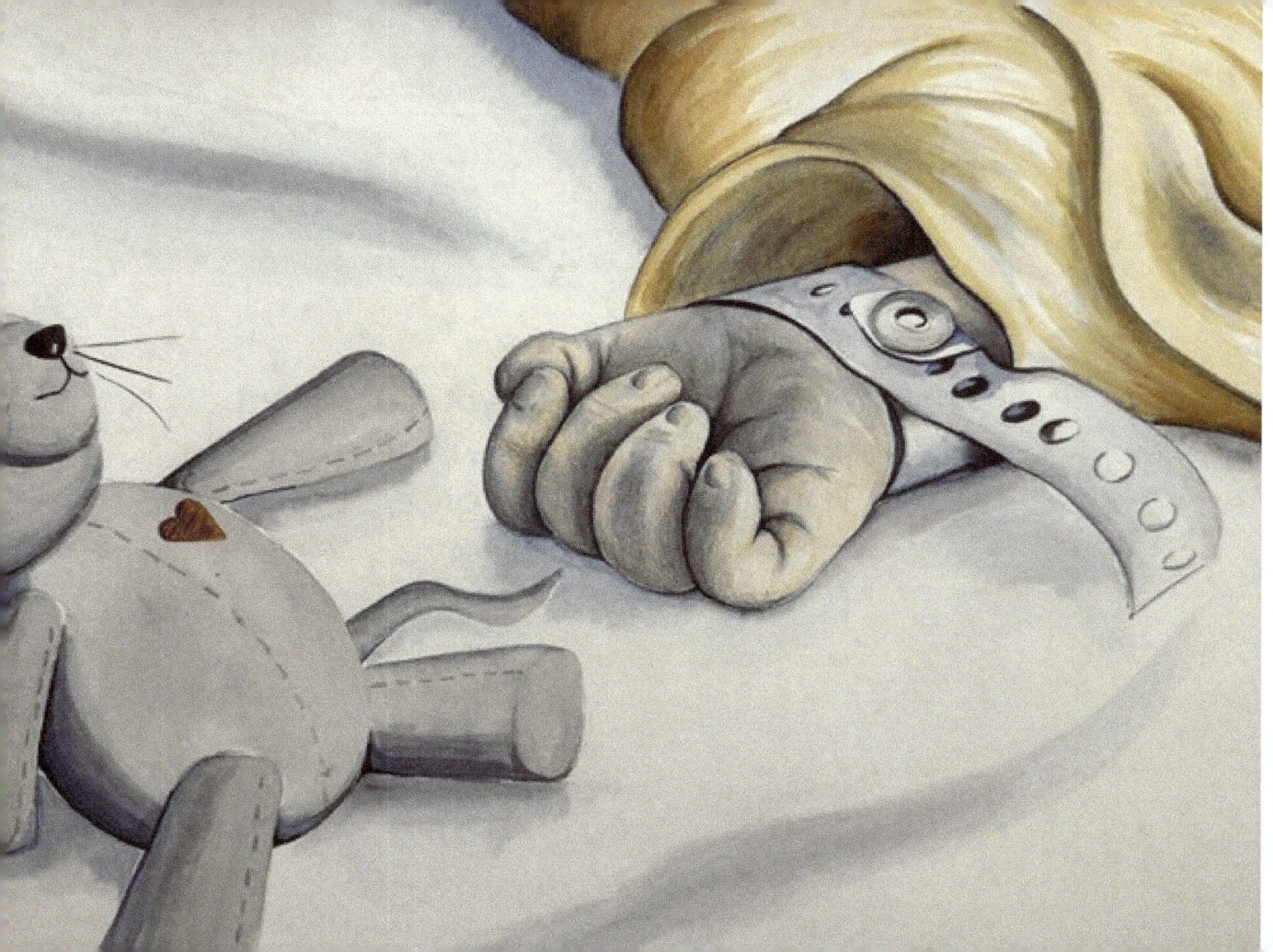

Whether you're small or you're grown,
your strength is your own
but the more you give,
the more you receive.

Of all of life's lessons,
this is the most important...

Whatever challenge you face...
... face it with the knowledge that you
can do amazing things!

With each hurdle that we leap (or stumble!) over
We learn and teach that each of us
is strong in our right.

When you feel small or tired, look in your heart and look to those care for you.
It's there that you'll find your strength.

Be proud of all the care, grace,
and strength you've shared.
This is how you make the world better!

You are amazing!
And the whole world is before you...

Waiting for you to shine your light upon it!

# All that We Learn...
## and Teach

Have you ever wondered what a tiny, fragile baby could teach a grown adult? In this inspiring book, you'll discover how even in the most challenging circumstances, there are invaluable lessons to be learned. Through spending time as a cuddler of the precious infants of the Neonatal Intensive Care Unit (NICU), Julie Senatore shares her insights on resilience, patience, and the power of love.

This book is a testament to the human spirit and a reminder that growth often occurs in the most unexpected places.

By *Julie Senatore*

ISBN 978-0-9970254-9-1

9 780997 025491